anythink

D0463312

Animal Spikes and Spines

Spines

Rebecca Rissman

Heinemann Library
Chicago, Illinois

www.heinemannraintree.com
Visit our website to find out more information about Heinemann-Raintree books.

To order:

☎ Phone 888-454-2279

🖥 Visit www.heinemannraintree.com to browse our catalog and order online.

Edited by Rebecca Rissman, Dan Nunn and Sian Smith
Designed by Joanna Hinton-Malivoire
Picture research by Tracy Cummins
Production by Victoria Fitzgerald
Originated by Capstone Global Library Ltd
Printed and bound in China by Leo Paper Products Ltd

15 14 13 12 11
10 9 8 7 6 5 4 3 2 1

Library of Congress Cataloging-in-Publication Data

Rissman, Rebecca.
  Spines / Rebecca Rissman.—1st ed.
      p. cm.—(Animal spikes and spines)
  Includes bibliographical references and index.
  ISBN 978-1-4329-5041-5 (hc)—ISBN 978-1-4329-5048-4 (pb)
1. Spines (Zoology)—Juvenile literature. I. Title.
QL385.R57 2012
591.47—dc22   2010044793

Acknowledgments
We would like to thank the following for permission to reproduce photographs: Getty Images pp **4** (Darrell Gulin), **9** & **10** (both Steven Hunt), **13** (Nacivet), **20** (Larry Dale Gordon), **22** (Nacivet); istockphoto pp **14** (© Anyka), **21** (© Daniel Laflor); National Geographic Stock pp **11** & **12** (both Paul Nicklen); Photolibrary pp **5** (Tim Jackson), **7** (Thorsten Milse), **8** (Max Gibbs), **15**, **16** & **23b** (all Brandon Cole); Shutterstock pp **6** (© F36lliuta Goean), **17** (© F3Connes), **18** (© Connes), **23a** (© F3Connes).

Cover photograph of a yellow spotted burrfish (Cyclichthys spilostylus) reproduced with permission of National Geographic Stock (Tim Laman). Back cover photograph of an iguana reproduced with permission of Shutterstock (© F3Connesx).

We would like to thank Michael Bright, Nancy Harris, Dee Reid, and Diana Bentley for their assistance in the preparation of this book.

Every effort has been made to contact copyright holders of material reproduced in this book. Any omissions will be rectified in subsequent printings if notice is given to the publisher.

Contents

Animal Body Parts

Animals have different body parts.

spines

Some animals have spines.

What Are Spines?

Spines are spiky body parts.

Some spines are made of bone.

Some spines are made of hard hairs.

Different Spines

Spines grow on different parts of animals' bodies.

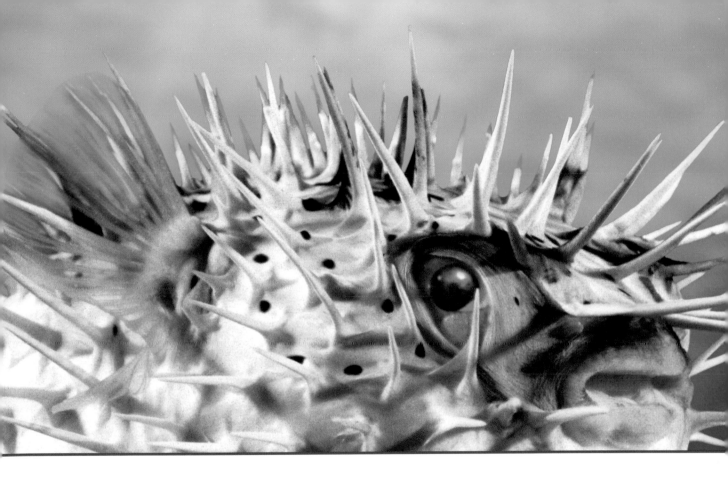

Some spines are short.

What animal is this?

This animal is a porcupine fish. Its spines tell animals not to eat it!

Some spines are colorful.

What animal is this?

This animal is a sea urchin.

Its spines tell fish to stay away.

Some spines are brown and white.

What animal is this?

This animal is a hedgehog. It rolls
into a spiny ball to keep safe.

Some spines are long and webbed.
What animal is this?

sail

This animal is a sailfish. Its spines hold up its tall sail.

Some spines are in long rows.
What animal is this?

This animal is an iguana. Its spines help to scare other animals away.

Your Body

Do you have spines?

No! You do not have spines.

Humans grow skin and hair on their bodies.

Can You Remember?

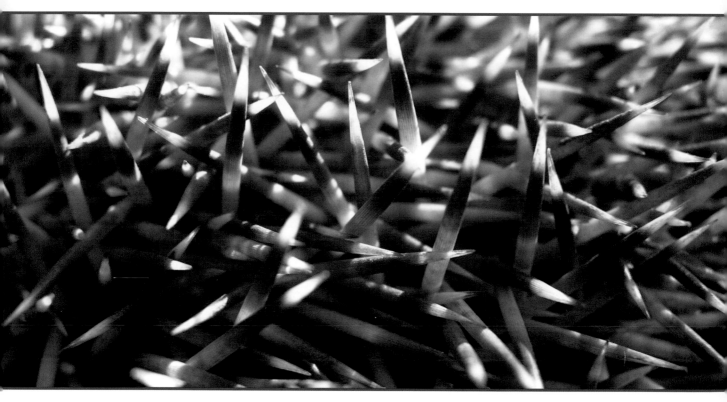

Which animal rolls into a spiny ball to keep safe?

Picture Glossary

spines sharp, pointed body parts that grow on an animal's body

webbed joined together by skin. Webbed feet have skin that joins the toes together.

Index

Notes for Parents and Teachers

Before reading

Show children the front cover of the book. Guide children in a discussion about what they think the book will be about. Tell children that spines are spiky body parts on animals. Can they think of animals that have spines? Then, discuss that spines are body parts and are used for different things.

After reading

Give out pictures of animals with spines (cut from magazines or printed from the internet). Ask the children to sort out animals with spines who live in the ocean from animals with spines who live on land. Help the children to create collages showing the variety of animals in each group. Encourage the children to compare the animals and to discuss the similarities and differences they find with a partner.